Anti-Money Laundering: What You Need to Know

Guernsey fiduciary edition

Susan Grossey

ISBN: 1496007220
ISBN-13: 978-1496007223

Illustrations by Chris Priestley

Susan's blog:
www.ihatemoneylaundering.wordpress.com

Susan's website:
www.thinkingaboutcrime.com

Susan's other books:
📖 "Money Laundering: A Training Strategy"
📖 "The Money Laundering Officer's Practical Handbook", 2006-2019
📖 "Anti-Money Laundering: A Guide for the Non-Executive Director", editions for UK, Guernsey, Jersey, Isle of Man and International
📖 "Fatal Forgery", "The Man in the Canary Waistcoat", "Worm in the Blossom", "Portraits of Pretence", "Faith, Hope and Trickery" and "Heir Apparent" – historical financial crime novels

Susan's e-books:
"Suspicious Activity: The Adventures of an MLRO", Parts 1 to 6

DEDICATION

To Trevor Millington OBE (1958-2012):
a leading light and tireless campaigner in the world of
asset forfeiture and proceeds of crime legislation

CONTENTS

ACKNOWLEDGMENTS

Thanks firstly to all the fiduciary sector staff who asked me the questions that form the basis of this book.

Thanks then to Paul who said, "You know what? You should write a book about it."

And lastly, thanks to all the fantastic MLROs, compliance officers, regulators and law enforcement agents who – over the many years I have worked in AML – have taught me pretty much everything I know.

INTRODUCTION

This short book is intended to provide anyone who works in a firm providing fiduciary services in Guernsey with an understanding of what money laundering is, why it matters so much, and what is being done in Guernsey and elsewhere to protect the fiduciary sector from contamination by criminal money.

It is not intended to take the place of your in-house anti-money laundering policy and procedures, which have been written specifically for your firm, but rather to put them into context and to explain why they are so vital – and why we ask you to do your very best to abide by them and implement them on a daily basis.

You are not expected to have an in-depth knowledge of money laundering and terrorist financing and their prevention and detection: having such in-depth knowledge is the job of your Money Laundering Compliance Officer and Money Laundering Reporting Officer. However, they can only do their jobs properly with your help, and this book will explain to you where their responsibility ends and yours begins, and how you can work together to safeguard yourselves, your firm, the fiduciary sector and the financial system.

1 WHAT IS MONEY LAUNDERING?

> The definition of money laundering is very simple: money laundering is the process by which criminals attempt to conceal the fact that their assets have come from crime.

Criminals are keen to do this because legislation is in place around the world to ensure that if someone is convicted of a crime, their proceeds of crime can be confiscated by the authorities – this is known as criminal forfeiture. Many jurisdictions (including Guernsey) now also have a civil forfeiture regime, which means that if someone is suspected of criminality but has yet to be charged or convicted, the authorities can apply to the courts to have that person's assets seized on the grounds that there is no legitimate provenance or explanation for them and therefore they must be the proceeds of crime. Fully aware of this, criminals want to disguise their proceeds of crime and put them beyond the reach of forfeiture.

What makes it difficult is that there is an infinite number of ways in which criminals can do this, and there is no typical money laundering scheme. However, it is generally accepted that there are different stages in the money laundering process, and the most common of these are:

Placement: In this initial stage, the criminal puts (or places) his criminal assets into the financial sector. At this point these assets are usually cash, and so the most vulnerable at this stage are those businesses that accept cash, such as retail banks, bureaux de change and casinos.   (Also at risk are those of your clients who accept cash, such as those already mentioned, plus businesses like taxi firms, hairdressers, takeaway food outlets and nail bars.)   However, not all money laundering requires this initial placement stage, as some crimes (such as tax evasion, corruption and many frauds) involve misappropriating assets that are already in the financial system. It would therefore be wrong to think that just because a business does not accept cash it cannot be used for money laundering.

Layering: The layering stage is when criminals move their assets around within the financial sector – moving them between accounts and financial products, between institutions and between jurisdictions – in order to make them hard to follow. Their goal is to make it difficult to find the assets and then, if they are found, to make it vexatious to seize them.   Any business that moves value around in any form is at risk of being used for layering purposes. Particularly useful to launderers are those businesses that can move value internationally – as can most firms which provide fiduciary services – as this allows the criminal to take advantage of differing jurisdictional standards of AML legislation and the slow pace of international financial investigations.

Integration: The final stage of money laundering is integration, when the criminal decides that his assets now look clean enough for him to bring them back into the legitimate economy so that he can use them as he wishes. Any business that facilitates "conversion" of any sort – such as a bank balance being turned into a property, or shares being turned into a bank balance, or an inheritance being subsumed into a trust – could be used to help with integration.

Although it is useful to understand and recognise these terms, it is rarely crucial to know whether you have been duped into layering the criminal's money or integrating it – as far as the law is concerned, it is all money laundering. Reading case studies can be helpful (some are given in the later chapter on *Red flags and case studies*), as they show you just how creative criminals can be and how the fiduciary sector can be targeted by them, but the best definition to keep in mind is that first one: money laundering is how criminals try to make their criminal proceeds look legal.

It is also important to remember that, in their quest to look clean, criminals need to build a cover story. They have to make themselves look and sound like, for instance, legitimate businessmen or beneficiaries of a will or big winners at a casino; after all, if they are to make people believe that their assets are not criminal, they need to have a good alternative explanation. And one way they create and maintain this alternative (false) explanation is by associating with, and profiting from the good reputation of, respected firms such as yours.

So do be aware that even if a client seems to have no desire at all to do anything that could be construed as placement, layering or integration – perhaps he simply pays your firm a professional retainer – he could be using you to form part of his cover story. Helping him to look legitimate when he is not could be considered to be money laundering (one of the money laundering offences is that of assisting someone to launder money), and it will certainly do your personal and corporate reputation no good at all.

What is terrorist financing?

Terrorist financing – and particularly its prevention and detection – has been of growing importance to the financial sector since the attacks on New York and Washington DC in September 2001. Various attempts have been made to define and outlaw it, with differing degrees of success.

From the point of view of prevention, the general response has been to add terrorist financing to existing money laundering legislation, requiring businesses covered by AML requirements to extend their efforts to what has been dubbed "CFT" – countering the financing of terrorism. So in Guernsey, for example, Schedule 3 to the Criminal Justice (Proceeds of Crime) (Bailiwick of Guernsey) Law, 1999 now requires specified businesses, including those in the fiduciary sector, to put in place procedures to prevent and forestall both money laundering and terrorist financing.

The actual offence of terrorist financing itself is found in several linked pieces of legislation and has two main definitions: money generated by acts of terrorism, and money intended for use in acts in terrorism. In practical terms, the first sort is rarer: terrorist organisations (unlike criminal organisations) do not exist to make money. And the second sort is extremely hard to spot because it is very small in volume: you do not need much money to commit an act of terrorism. The attack on the London transport system in July 2005, for example, cost its organisers just over £7,200. However, despite its small volume, the impact of terrorist financing can be devastating.

Although they are often grouped together as "ML/TF", there are differences between money laundering and terrorist financing. The main one is that money laundering involves taking dirty money and trying to make it look clean, while the majority of terrorist financing involves taking clean money and using it for dirty purposes. (Most terrorism is funded by money that has been earned legitimately and donated willingly.)

However, there is one key way in which terrorist financiers do resemble money launderers: both groups want to use the world's financial system to move money around while revealing as little information as possible that might enable the true source, destination or purpose of that money to be discovered. It is therefore both essential and logical that your firm's AML efforts have been extended to encompass CFT as well.

> From here on, to make this book more readable, I will refer only to "AML" and "money laundering" – please understand that I actually mean "AML/CFT" and "money laundering and terrorist financing".

World bodies

AML measures have developed over time – they did not spring up fully formed. Various agencies have had their say in this process of development, and entire books have been written about the genesis of our current AML legal and regulatory framework, but the main players in today's world of AML are these.

> Links to the agencies and legislation mentioned in this book are given in the final chapter on *Useful sources of information*.

Financial Action Task Force

The Financial Action Task Force (FATF) is the international body devoted to developing and promoting policies to combat money laundering. It was established in 1989 under the umbrella of the Organisation of Economic Co-operation and Development (OECD) and currently has thirty-seven member jurisdictions. Being an FATF member jurisdiction means that you sign up to their standards, and also agree to do your bit in promoting those standards outside the membership.

Although Guernsey is not a member of the FATF, as a Crown Dependency of the United Kingdom (which is a member) it has a close association with the FATF and tends to follow its standards.

The FATF's AML standards are expressed in the form of Recommendations. These Recommendations are written as a guide for governments on how to formulate their AML framework, including Recommendations on legislation, supervision and international co-operation. They started out in 1990 as the Forty Recommendations, and were augmented in 2001 by Nine Special Recommendations on Terrorist Financing. They were updated in February 2012, to take account of recent developments in the world of AML/CFT, and rationalised into the neat Forty again.

The FATF also runs a continuous programme of mutual evaluation of its member jurisdictions. Each is examined in turn on the basis of an on-site visit conducted by a team of experts from other member countries, who use an approved and published handbook to guide their review. The resulting report assesses the extent to which the evaluated country has moved forward in implementing an effective AML system, and highlights areas in which further progress can still be made. These reports – and particularly their executive summaries which outline the main areas of interest and concern – are used extensively by Money Laundering Compliance Officers (MLCOs) and Money Laundering Reporting Officers (MLROs) to help them understand the money laundering risks posed by particular jurisdictions, and so adjust their risk-based approach. (As explained in the later chapter on *The risk-based approach*, jurisdictional risk is an important element of overall risk.) An FATF member jurisdiction can expect to be reviewed every three to four years.

As well as the FATF itself, there are numerous "FATF-style regional bodies", which do much the same work in specific areas of the world. Examples are the MENAFATF in the Middle East and north Africa, and the CFATF in the Caribbean.

MONEYVAL

MONEYVAL was established in 1997 by the Council of Europe. Its initial main responsibility was to conduct AML/CFT evaluations of those Council of Europe member states that are not members of the FATF, thereby ensuring that every Council of Europe member state, whether a member of the FATF or not, would be subject to an ongoing cycle of evaluations. Now, however, MONEYVAL also conducts AML/CFT evaluations of other jurisdictions – including, from 2014 onwards, Guernsey. Like the FATF reviewers, MONEYVAL reviewers use the approved FATF methodology and handbook when conducting their reviews.

It is MONEYVAL that now conducts evaluations of Guernsey's AML/CFT regime. Earlier evaluations of Guernsey's regime (up to the one published in January 2011) were conducted by the International Monetary Fund.

International Monetary Fund

In April 2001 the International Monetary Fund announced that it would become more involved in the global fight against money laundering. It launched its own programme of assessments of the AML/CFT regimes of over forty-five countries – once again using the approved FATF methodology and handbook. It often conducts ongoing evaluations jointly with the FATF.

2 GUERNSEY AML LEGISLATION IN OUTLINE

Like nearly all jurisdictions, Guernsey tackles the problem of money laundering from two directions.

First it has legislation containing the main money laundering offences and terrorist financing offences: the Criminal Justice (Proceeds of Crime) (Bailiwick of Guernsey) Law, 1999; the Disclosure (Bailiwick of Guernsey) Law, 2007; and the Terrorism and Crime (Bailiwick of Guernsey) Law, 2002.

And second, it has legislation requiring certain businesses (including your firm) to put in place procedures to prevent and forestall money laundering and terrorist financing: Schedule 3 to the Criminal Justice (Proceeds of Crime) (Bailiwick of Guernsey) Law, 1999 (as amended).

Criminal Justice (Proceeds of Crime) (Bailiwick of Guernsey) Law, 1999

The Criminal Justice (Proceeds of Crime) (Bailiwick of Guernsey) Law, 1999 (henceforward "the Criminal Justice Law") is a large piece of legislation, but for now we are concerned only with the four individual money laundering offences that it contains. The fifth individual money laundering offence is found in the Disclosure (Bailiwick of Guernsey) Law, 2007.

All five of these offences apply to the proceeds of any crime that constitutes an indictable (i.e. serious) offence in the Bailiwick or that (if committed overseas) would constitute such an offence in the Bailiwick if it occurred there. There is no *de minimis* and no statute of limitations, so the money laundering offences involve the proceeds of any serious criminal behaviour, by anyone, at any time, anywhere. It is true "all crimes" legislation.

Concealing or transferring

You commit this offence if you conceal, disguise, convert or transfer criminal proceeds, or remove them from the Bailiwick.

The only statutory defences (i.e. defences allowed by the law itself) are to make a "disclosure" of your suspicion that the proceeds are from crime – in other words, to make a report to your MLRO (or, if you are the MLRO, to the Financial Intelligence Service, or FIS) – or to have a reasonable excuse for not making such a disclosure (see *Failure to disclose*, below, for more on this). If found guilty, you could be given an unlimited fine or a prison sentence of up to fourteen years or both.

Assisting

You commit this offence if you enter into or become concerned in an arrangement which you know or suspect facilitates the retention or control of criminal proceeds by or on behalf of another person, or if you use that person's criminal proceeds to make a loan to him or to make investments on his behalf. The drafting of this offence is such that no actual value has to move: simply giving advice could be sufficient to commit this offence, which is a danger area for professional firms such as yours.

Again, the only statutory defences are that you made a disclosure to your MLRO or had a reasonable excuse for not doing so. And again, the penalties are an unlimited fine or a prison sentence of up to fourteen years or both.

Acquisition, possession or use

You commit this offence if you acquire, possess or use criminal property.

Again, making a disclosure to the MLRO or having a reasonable excuse for not doing so are allowed as statutory defences. In addition, you can show that you acquired or gained use or possession of the criminal property for an "adequate consideration" (i.e. a fair market price) and so had no reason to suspect its criminal origins. Once again, the penalties are an unlimited fine or a prison sentence of up to fourteen years or both.

Tipping off

You commit this offence if you know or suspect that a money laundering disclosure has been made (either internally to the MLRO or externally to the FIS), or that a money laundering investigation is underway or about to start, and then you tell any other person about that disclosure or investigation.

In November 2011, Guernsey's HM Procureur issued guidance on the tipping off offence, in which he clarified that sharing information about a disclosure within an organisation would not necessarily constitute tipping off, as long as the information was shared in order to meet AML requirements, and as long as the spread of the information was controlled by the MLRO. Therefore, to guard against tipping off, your MLRO will always make sure that information about money laundering disclosures is shared on a strictly "need to know" basis. And if you personally ever make a disclosure, you must not tell anyone that you have done so without first checking with the MLRO that you are allowed to tell them.

The main defence against tipping off is to be able to demonstrate that you shared the information entirely in accordance with the law. The penalties for tipping off are an unlimited fine or a prison sentence of up to five years or both.

Disclosure (Bailiwick of Guernsey) Law, 2007

The Disclosure (Bailiwick of Guernsey) Law, 2007 (henceforward "the Disclosure Law") contains

Guernsey's fifth individual money laundering offence: failure to disclose.

Failure to disclose

You commit this offence if you know or suspect, or have reasonable grounds for knowing or suspecting, that someone is engaged in money laundering (or terrorist financing), and you find out about this in the course of the business of a financial services business or a non-financial services business, and then you do not report your suspicion in the form of a disclosure to your MLRO (or, if you are the MLRO, to the FIS).

You will spot that phrase "reasonable grounds". This means that the court will apply the objective (as opposed to subjective) test of suspicion; in short, the prosecution will not have to prove that you *did* know or suspect that there was money laundering going on, but only that you *should have* known or suspected. The court will compare your behaviour to an objective standard: did you demonstrate the level of vigilance and understanding that would be expected of someone doing your sort of job, at your sort of level, in your sort of firm, with your type and length of experience? Obviously, this means that the test will be applied more harshly to more senior staff – and your MLCO, MLRO and directors will be expected to have the highest standards of behaviour of all.

There are two main statutory defences to this offence. First, you can show that you had a reasonable excuse for not making a disclosure – perhaps you were taken to hospital as an emergency admission just before you were about to submit your disclosure. (However, what would be considered reasonable has never been tested in court, so proceed with care.) And second, there is what is known as the training defence, whereby you say that you did not make a disclosure because no-one had told you how to or perhaps you had not even been told that you are expected to make disclosures.

The penalties for failure to disclose are an unlimited fine or a prison sentence of up to five years or both.

Terrorism and Crime (Bailiwick of Guernsey) Law, 2002

The Terrorism and Crime (Bailiwick of Guernsey) Law, 2002 (henceforward "the Terrorism and Crime Law") contains several individual money laundering offences (all carrying a maximum prison sentence of fourteen years, apart from five years for the last one):

- fund raising for terrorist purposes

- using or possessing money or terrorist property for the purpose of terrorism

- entering into or becoming concerned in an funding arrangement when you know or have reasonable grounds to suspect will be used for the purpose of terrorism

- concealing or transferring terrorist property

- (for insurers) making or authorising a payment under an insurance contract taken out against payments made in response to terrorist demands

- failing to disclose knowledge or suspicion of terrorist financing.

If the authorities are certain that the money involved is linked to terrorism, they will bring charges under these offences. If they are certain that the money is not connected with terrorism, or are not sure where it is from, they will bring charges under the Criminal Justice Law or the Disclosure Law, as outlined above.

Schedule 3 to the Criminal Justice (Proceeds of Crime) (Bailiwick of Guernsey) Law, 1999

Previously Guernsey's AML/CFT obligations were contained in two sets of Regulations (one set for financial services businesses and the other for prescribed businesses). However, they are now housed in Schedule 3 to the Criminal Justice (Proceeds of Crime) (Bailiwick of Guernsey) Law, 1999 (henceforward "Schedule 3"), which came into force on 31 March 2019.

These AML/CFT obligations were not conjured out of nothing: they are Guernsey's domestic response to the standards set in the EU's Money Laundering Directives. Although Guernsey is not an EU Member State, and therefore is under no obligation to transpose EU legislation into its domestic legislation, when it comes to AML issues Guernsey prefers to adhere to the high international standards set by the EU in the form of its Directives. We are currently operating under the Fifth European Money Laundering Directive; when a new Directive comes into force, Guernsey will almost certainly update its own legislation.

The AML/CFT obligations of Schedule 3 apply to what are known as "specified businesses", which covers both financial services businesses and prescribed businesses.

Financial services businesses are defined more fully at Schedule 1 to the Criminal Justice Law and include:

- lending institutions

- money service businesses

- traders in bullion or postage stamps

- those operating informal money transfer networks

- those trading in investments of any kind

- money brokers and money changers

- deposit-taking institutions

- investment businesses

- insurance companies

- fiduciaries.

Prescribed businesses are defined more fully at Schedule 2 to the Criminal Justice Law and include:

- those providing legal services

- those providing accountancy services

- estate agents

- high value dealers (i.e. those trading in goods for cash payments totalling £7,500 or more)

- casinos and organised gambling facilities.

Any specified business covered by Schedule 3 is required to put in place the four components of an AML regime: customer due diligence procedures; record-keeping procedures; internal reporting procedures; and staff training procedures. Exactly who is responsible within your firm for making sure that this is done is the subject of the next chapter of this book.

Guidance

To help your firm to comply with the Criminal Justice Law, the Terrorism and Crime Law, the Disclosure Law and Schedule 3 (as well as other related legislation), the Guernsey Financial Services Commission (GFSC) has issued the *Handbook on Countering Financial Crime and Terrorist Financing*.

This handbook offers assistance with compliance with legislation, and provides a blueprint against which that compliance can be judged. Your MLCO will be familiar with the handbook, and should ensure that your in-house AML/CFT procedures comply with the handbook at all times.

3 THE KEY AML RESPONSIBILITIES

Sometimes people think that all AML responsibility lies with the MLCO and the MLRO. Certainly they have a lot to do with it, but they do not – and indeed cannot – act alone. In fact, AML responsibility within your firm is shared by everyone.

Overseeing your firm's AML regime is your Board of directors. They are responsible for putting in place and then monitoring and reviewing the AML regime, and for signing off on its appropriateness, proportionality and effectiveness.

The MLCO is primarily responsible for making sure that the AML regime is implemented on a daily basis. And the MLRO is responsible for receiving and reacting to internal disclosures of suspicion of money laundering or terrorist financing. The roles of MLCO and MLRO may be held by the same person or by different individuals.

If there is ever a failure in your firm's AML regime – if, for instance, it is found that customer due diligence is not being performed correctly, or that staff training is not of a sufficient quality – then the question asked by the court and the regulator will be this: was it a failure of oversight (and therefore the responsibility of the Board), or a failure of implementation (and therefore the responsibility of the MLCO or of the MLRO)?

The MLCO

The Money Laundering Compliance Officer has responsibility for your firm's compliance with its AML/CFT policies, procedures and controls. His key functions include:

- overseeing the monitoring and testing of the AML/CFT regime to assess its appropriateness and effectiveness

- investigating any matters of concern or non-compliance with the regime

- making periodic reports to the Board on compliance matters, and

- keeping up to date with money laundering and terrorist financing trends and techniques, so that the risk-based approach of the AML/CFT regime can be adjusted to take account of diminishing or increasing areas of risk.

The MLRO

The Money Laundering Reporting Officer is responsible for dealing with disclosures of suspected money laundering and terrorist financing. His key functions are:

- to receive reports of suspected money laundering and terrorist financing from members of staff – these are known as internal disclosures

- to make enquiries into those internal disclosures and to keep careful records of his enquiries

- to pass on to the authorities (in Guernsey, the Financial Intelligence Service, or FIS) those disclosures about which he remains suspicious after his enquiries – these are then known as external disclosures.

Your firm will also have a "nominated officer" to undertake the duties of the MLRO when the MLRO is absent.

You

Between them, the Board, the MLCO and the MLRO can assemble and maintain your firm's AML regime, which consists of an AML policy and the AML procedures.

The AML policy is simply a statement of your firm's commitment to AML.

The AML procedures contain all the details about how this is to be achieved, covering the four main components as set out in Schedule 3: customer due diligence procedures; record-keeping procedures; internal reporting procedures; and staff training procedures.

However, both the policy and the procedures are only theory until someone puts them into practice – and that is you (and your colleagues, of course).

Under your terms of employment, you undertake to understand, uphold and comply with your firm's procedures (of all sorts, not just AML procedures – but definitely including them).

As a member of the professional financial community, you are expected to do all you can to preserve Guernsey's good name and to protect its financial sector from criminal infiltration and abuse. This is best achieved by ensuring that you apply professional diligence and vigilance in every aspect of your work.

And as you are affected personally by the Criminal Justice Law, following your firm's AML procedures is a sensible way to ensure that you do not unwittingly become involved in a money laundering scheme.

Obviously a book like this cannot go into details for each individual firm providing fiduciary services, and so you will need to read this alongside the specific AML policy and procedures that are in place for your firm.

For your own protection, it is important that you understand fully and follow closely the obligations placed on you by your own firm's AML policy and procedures. If there is anything in that AML policy or those AML procedures that you do not understand, or if you think that something is wrong or missing, you should raise it with your MLCO.

4 THE RISK-BASED APPROACH TO AML

When Guernsey's AML regime was first introduced, it was a fairly rigid structure. With regard to due diligence, it was sufficient for firms to apply the same level of checking to most of their clients. Since then, and with the benefit of being able to assess the effectiveness of such an regime, world bodies – led by the FATF – have come to the conclusion that we need to have a more flexible approach. In short, we need to underpin all aspects of our AML regime with a risk-based approach.

With a risk-based approach (or RBA), you can adjust the level of due diligence that you apply to a client on the basis of the money laundering and/or terrorist financing risk that you think they present. In other words, if you judge that a client is very unlikely to be involved in money laundering or terrorist financing, you can perform a lower level of due diligence on them, but if you think that they are particularly risky, you need to mitigate that risk by undertaking a higher level of due diligence.

Why should we have an RBA?

There are several benefits to applying the RBA. Firstly, it recognises that not all clients are created equal, and that some – by dint of their very nature, or their location, or their line of business, or the products and services they choose to use – present you with a higher risk of money laundering and/or terrorist financing. Secondly, it gives your Board and MLCO the flexibility to devise the AML regime that best fits your firm and your clients – thus enabling your firm to take advantage of the understanding that it has built up of its own market and the risks inherent in it. And thirdly, it allows you to prioritise your effort where it will have the best results; in other words, you will be encouraged to spend more time doing more checks on more risky clients, and less time doing fewer checks on less risky clients – which should be more cost-effective, more efficient and ultimately more rewarding.

Applying the RBA

When the MLCO is designing your firm's AML procedures, and the Board is checking and approving them, they all need to be happy that those procedures have taken the RBA into account. They need to ensure that the procedures have allowed for the four elements of risk (and throughout this book "risk" means purely money laundering and terrorist financing risk – not credit risk or any other sort of risk), which are:

Client risk: for instance, a multi-national company owned by another company owned by a trust that was settled by a foundation is inherently more risky than a locally-resident granny – and client risk should also consider the risk associated with any beneficial owner of the client

Country/territory risk: some jurisdictions are declared by regulatory decree to be high risk (listed in Appendix H and Appendix I to the GFSC *Handbook*), while others are pinpointed by international indices, and still others are considered to have an AML regime equivalent to that of Guernsey (listed in Appendix C to the *Handbook*) – the client's connection with certain countries or territories will affect his risk profile

Product/service/transaction risk: certain products, services and transactions are more attractive to money launderers and terrorist financiers than others – anything that can disguise ownership or allow easy international transfer of value will be high on their shopping list

Delivery channel risk: it is more risky to have a client you have never met or with whom you deal only remotely than one you meet regularly and deal with face-to-face.

The purpose of measuring a client against these four risk elements is to ascertain what overall level of risk he presents, so that your firm can then mitigate that risk by applying the correct level of due diligence.

It is entirely up to your firm to decide how many categories of risk are appropriate to your range of clients, but most find that three categories – low risk, medium or standard risk, and high risk – are perfectly sufficient.

There are some clients whom you are not permitted to have at all, regardless of the level of risk that you may consider them to present. They are therefore totally outside the RBA. These are individuals and organisations that feature on international sanctions lists and are thereby denied access to the world's financial systems. Checking at the outset that a potential client is not sanctioned, and then monitoring them throughout the relationship to make sure that they do not become sanctioned, is a vital part of the customer due diligence process, as described in the next chapter.

The need for constant revision

As the whole purpose of the RBA is to ensure that your in-house risk mitigation procedures reflect the current risks, it is essential regularly to re-visit your RBA and check that it is still appropriate and proportionate to the current risks facing your firm and Guernsey. The ways in which criminals and terrorists operate, the sectors and jurisdictions that they target, and the products and services on offer to them are all changing constantly, and an RBA that was appropriate a decade ago will be sadly outdated today.

If you are involved in the review of client relationships, you may well find that you are asked to contribute to this assessment of the RBA, as you will be in a good position to see whether what your firm is doing to guard against money laundering and terrorist financing is still meeting that need.

5 CUSTOMER DUE DILIGENCE

To recap, Schedule 3 requires firms providing fiduciary services to put in place the four components of an AML regime: customer due diligence procedures; record-keeping procedures; internal reporting procedures; and staff training procedures. We will now look at these in turn, and the first of them is customer due diligence.

> At the end of each of the next five chapters there is a blank box where you can note down anything you would like to find out more about, by consulting your firm's AML procedures or by asking the MLCO or MLRO. If anything occurs to you as you are reading, be sure to jot it down before you forget it.

Customer due diligence (CDD) used to be known as Know Your Client (KYC). But with the introduction of the RBA and the general modernisation of AML, it was recognised that the accepted definition of KYC was no longer broad enough. CDD encompasses

KYC, and then extends beyond it into knowing your client's business and even – in some very high-risk situations – knowing your client's clients, as well as including ongoing monitoring of the client.

As explained earlier, the main point of the RBA is to ensure that you meet money laundering risk with the appropriate and proportionate level of due diligence to mitigate that risk. The three terms used in Schedule 3 for the most common levels of due diligence are customer due diligence (CDD – the standard level), simplified customer due diligence (SCDD – the reduced level that can be used in certain low-risk situations) and enhanced customer due diligence (ECDD – the higher level required in high-risk situations).

The CDD procedures in your firm will take you (or whoever is responsible for taking on new clients or maintaining your firm's relationships with those clients) through four steps:

- assessing the proposed client's level of risk according to your firm's RBA

- clarifying what level of due diligence must then be applied

- specifying how that due diligence requirement can be fulfilled for that type of client, and

- specifying how the requirement for ongoing due diligence can be met.

Assessing risk

Your firm has a process for assessing the money laundering risk presented by your clients. This may be a form that is completed in consultation with the client and then reviewed by someone trained to assess risk. It may be a matrix – either manual or computerised – into which the proposed client's details are entered and which then calculates the appropriate risk category. Whatever method is used, for each and every client there needs to be a record of how the decision was reached on which risk category was appropriate.

(Of course, your firm is also assessing clients for other sorts of risk such as credit risk. And your money laundering and terrorist financing risk analysis may well form part of that wider risk analysis – but in order to comply with Schedule 3 your firm has to be able to demonstrate that you looked *specifically* at money laundering and terrorist financing risks.)

A client's risk category is not static: their profile or activity may change, and the background against which they operate will certainly change. This is why monitoring has become so important to the RBA, as discussed further on in this chapter, and checking that the client still has the appropriate risk rating is an important component of that monitoring.

Due diligence specifics

This book cannot go into the specifics of your firm's procedures, but there are certain elements of CDD that are common to all firms providing fiduciary services, and these are outlined below.

Enhanced measures

Schedule 3 also requires that – regardless of the risk category to which you assign a client and the level of CDD that accompanies that risk category – you must then look again at the client and determine whether any aspect of the relationship or transaction would require "enhanced measures" to be taken, over and above the level of CDD (whether simplified, standard or enhanced). Enhanced measures must be taken when the relationship or transaction involves a client who:

- is not resident in the Bailiwick, or

- is using private banking services, or

- is a legal person or arrangement used for personal asset holding purposes, or

- has – or is owned by a legal person which has – nominee shareholders.

If a client falls into a category which requires enhanced measures, you will need to follow the enhanced measures set out in your CDD procedures. The specific enhanced measures that you will need to apply will focus on the element of the relationship that has caused the client to become eligible for enhanced measures in the first place – it is unlikely that every aspect of the relationship will be subject to enhanced measures.

Verification of individual identity

The starting point for all due diligence is the verification of individual identity. All clients (even the most complex multinational corporations) are made up of individuals, and knowing who they are is the bedrock of all due diligence.

For individual clients (and this definition also includes any individual acting on behalf of the client)

Schedule 3 requires require you to verify (i.e. prove to the best of your professional ability) an individual's name, residential address and date of birth. For all but low risk individual clients, you must also verify their place of birth and nationality (or nationalities, if they hold more than one).

There are certain documents that you can use to do this (such as a current passport and a recent utility bill) and the documents that are acceptable and the number of corroborating documents that you need to collect will depend on the level of due diligence that you are applying.

All the permutations will be set out in your firm's CDD procedures. These will explain, for each and every type of client that you have or are likely to get, what you need to do to meet the requirements of normal, simplified and enhanced customer due diligence and – where appropriate – enhanced measures. As well as the standard client types – individual, corporate, etc. – there will be procedures for dealing with more unusual cases, such as the financially excluded (who may not have the usual forms of identity document) and minors (who may not yet have any documents in their own name). If you come across a client who does not fit into any of the categories, or if you are not sure which category applies, you should take up the matter with your MLCO; this is too important to just guess at or – worse – ignore.

Your procedures will also explain about the importance of copy certification. When you keep copies of due diligence documents for your records, it is not sufficient to have plain photocopies: you need to have certified copies. In other words, someone on whom you are permitted to rely (and this will be specified in your procedures) makes the copy, and certifies on it that they saw the original document and (for photographic documents) the person to whom it belongs. If there is ever an enquiry, it will then be obvious from the certified copy who it was who saw the original document, and perhaps met the client, and when.

Your CDD procedures will also explain that you need to verify the identity of all parties to a joint account, and that if there are beneficial owners involved (see *Beneficial owners*, below) you must verify their identities as well.

Clients will sometimes be impatient – or perhaps even downright intimidating – when you are making due diligence enquiries. They may simply be tired of providing information to institutions, or they may actually have something to hide. Whatever their motivation, your job remains the same: you must ask and get answers to the due diligence questions, and obtain the underlying documents that you need to verify those answers. If you cannot get the information you need about them in order to verify their identity and enable a risk assessment to be done, your firm cannot take them on (or retain them) as a client.

Enhanced customer due diligence for individuals

If an individual client is deemed by your RBA to be high risk, you will need to apply ECDD. Precisely what form that ECDD takes will be specified in your firm's CDD procedures, which will be based on the requirements of the legislation. Schedule 3 sets out the elements of ECDD, which include obtaining senior management sign-off on the relationship, taking reasonable measures to establish and understand the client's source of funds and source of wealth, and carrying out more frequent and more intensive monitoring of the relationship.

Verification of legal entities

Your firm's CDD procedures for the verification of legal entities will of necessity be lengthy, but thankfully each type of legal entity follows the same pattern. What you will need to ascertain in each case is:

- the identity of the legal structure itself, and

- the identity of those individuals with ownership of or control over the legal structure's affairs.

Verification of the identity of the structure will be achieved through sight of certain documents (Certificate of Incorporation for a company, Deed of Partnership for a partnership, trust deed for a trust and so on). Again, certified copies must be kept.

Your firm's CDD procedures for legal entities will cover all possible structures, e.g. companies (public and private), partnerships, trusts, charities, schools and colleges, clubs and societies, public sector bodies, etc.

Pinpointing the key individuals, prior to verifying their identity, is often the trickiest part of the process, and you may well need to ask the MLCO for some guidance as you get used to doing this. It may help to be aware of the key responsibilities (decision-making, control of the assets, and interface with your firm) that will be most attractive to criminals and that they would most like to take over.

The number of key individuals (for example, how many members of a Board to verify, when all can be said to have some control over the structure, or how many trustees to verify) will depend on the risk category of the client, as the purpose of the exercise is to do enough CDD to mitigate the risk presented by that client. Again, the MLCO will be able to help you with this.

Simplified customer due diligence for legal entities

If a client is itself an "Appendix C business", you are permitted by Schedule 3 to apply simplified customer due diligence. Appendix C businesses are:

- financial services businesses supervised by the GFSC

- businesses carried on from countries listed in Appendix C and which, were they in Guernsey, would be financial services businesses

- businesses carried on by lawyers and accountants in the UK, Guernsey, Jersey or the Isle of Man.

With Appendix C businesses, all you need to verify is that the business is indeed an Appendix C business, and that the individual with whom you are dealing is authorised to represent the business.

You do not have to apply SCDD in all such cases – it is still your firm's decision. And you certainly should not apply SCDD if, despite a business being an Appendix C business, you feel that it presents more than a low level of risk.

Enhanced customer due diligence for legal entities

If a legal entity client is deemed by your RBA to be high risk, you will need to apply ECDD. Precisely what form that ECDD takes will be specified in your firm's CDD procedures, which will be based on the requirements of the legislation and may well include looking more closely into the complexity of the legal structure and asking for documentary proof of certain key elements, and/or obtaining the most recent annual report and accounts and a list of directors/partners. As with individuals, you could do more frequent monitoring, or require senior management sign-off on the application.

Beneficial owners

Transparency of beneficial ownership is now more important than ever, as criminals have realised that an excellent way to launder money is to hide behind a respectable client and then control things from behind the scenes. To guard against this, firms providing fiduciary services must have procedures to ascertain whether a client has beneficial owners and, if it does, to identify them and take reasonable measures to verify their identity.

It is important to recognise that beneficial ownership extends beyond legal ownership and control to encompass ultimate ownership and control, down to the specific individuals who are calling the shots.

According to Schedule 3, the beneficial owner is the natural person who ultimately owns or controls the client, or the person on whose behalf the business relationship or occasional transaction is being conducted. For trusts and other legal arrangements, the beneficial owner is any beneficiary in whom an interest has been vested, or any person who appears likely to benefit from the legal arrangement. If you have any difficulty deciding whether there is a beneficial owner, or who that is, you should discuss the matter with your MLCO.

Politically Exposed Persons

You may well have heard of Politically Exposed Persons, or PEPs. In fact, there are three types of PEP: foreign PEPs, domestic PEPs and IOPEPs (PEPs who work for international organisations). A PEP is:

- a person who has, or has had, a prominent public function in a country or territory other than the Bailiwick (foreign PEP), or in the Bailiwick (domestic PEP), or within an international organisation (IOPEP), or

- an immediate family member of such a person, or

- a close associate of such a person.

In short, PEPs are those who have access to public influence and/or public money, and as such they (and their families and close associates) are more susceptible to corruption.

Ascertaining whether or not a client is a PEP in the first place brings its own challenges. You can ask the client. You can do Internet searches on them. And your firm may subscribe to commercial databases that will either screen your client list automatically, or allow you to do *ad hoc* searches as and when you have an application or review that warrants it.

Foreign PEPs

If a client is a foreign PEP (either in their own right or through family or business association with a foreign PEP), Schedule 3 requires that ECDD must be applied, and specifically that you:

- require senior management sign-off on the relationship with the foreign PEP

- take reasonable measures to establish and understand the foreign PEP's source of funds and source of wealth, and

- conduct enhanced ongoing monitoring on the relationship.

Once a foreign PEP leaves the role which conferred their PEP status, you can consider whether you need to continue applying PEP-related ECDD. If the PEP is very senior – a head of state, or has the power to direct the spending of significant funds – you can never remove their PEP status (nor that of their family and close associates). If neither of those applies, you may remove their PEP status (and that of their family and close associates) seven years after they have left the role, as long as you establish and understand their source of funds and source of wealth.

International Organisation PEPs

If a client is an IOPEP (either in their own right or through family or business association with an IOPEP), Schedule 3 requires that ECDD must be considered, taking into account the particular circumstances of the IOPEP's public function.

Once an IOPEP leaves the role which conferred their PEP status, you can consider whether you need to continue applying PEP-related ECDD. If the IOPEP is very senior – the head of an international organisation, or has the power to direct the spending of significant funds – you can never remove their PEP status (nor that of their family and close associates). If neither of those applies, you may remove their PEP status (and that of their family and close associates) seven years after they have left the role, as long as you understand their source of funds.

Domestic PEPs

If a client is a domestic PEP (either in their own right or through family or business association with a domestic PEP), Schedule 3 requires that ECDD must be considered, taking into account the particular circumstances of the domestic PEP's public function.

Once a domestic PEP leaves the role which conferred their PEP status, you can remove their PEP status (and that of their family and close associates) five years after they have left the role, as long as you understand their source of funds.

Sanctions

Just as some PEPs fall outside the RBA because you are told that they must always be considered high risk, so there are other individuals and entities that fall outside the RBA in its entirety because you are simply not permitted to have them as clients. It is a not a matter of applying super-ultra-enhanced customer due diligence to them: they are forbidden because they are subject to sanctions.

Sanctions are pieces of legislation which seek to limit behaviour. They are applied to individuals and organisations for many reasons. One of the main ones is to deny them access to the world's financial systems, which is done by imposing financial sanctions.

Rather than start from scratch and publish its own list of those who are subject to sanctions, Guernsey instead uses the main sanctions target list issued by the Office of Financial Sanctions Implementation within HM Treasury in the UK, and then adds to it any other targets of local sanctions legislation.

The OFSI list is a consolidated list of all individuals and entities mentioned in any sanctions (including financial sanctions) issued by the United Nations and/or the UK. The list is updated regularly – on average, about three times a week – and part of your firm's CDD obligations is to check the current list against your client database. This is done for every new applicant, and whenever a client transaction or relationship is reviewed. If a possible match is found, you must tell your MLRO who will then report the match immediately to the States of Guernsey Policy & Resources Committee. It is a criminal offence to start or maintain a relationship with, or process a transaction involving, a sanctioned individual or entity.

Your firm may also be covered by American sanctions lists, depending on your exposure to US jurisdictional reach. If the American sanctions list (maintained by part of the US Treasury called the Office of Foreign Assets Control) applies, again, your firm will be checking for matches amongst all existing clients and new applicants.

And although – since leaving the EU – the UK's sanctions regime has separated from the EU's sanctions regime, your firm may choose to comply with EU sanctions as well as those of the UK, particularly if you have exposure to the EU through your client base or your areas of activity.

Monitoring

Monitoring is now an integral and vital part of your firm's CDD. In fact, there are several types of AML monitoring going on: monitoring the money laundering and terrorist financing risks facing your firm and Guernsey; monitoring your RBA to make sure that it is still appropriate and proportionate to those risks; and monitoring the transactions and activity of your clients. The first two are more particularly the responsibility of your Board and MLCO, but the third – monitoring clients – forms part of the work of many people in your firm, probably including you.

The monitoring of clients is required by Schedule 3, and encompasses two activities: ongoing monitoring, and regular reviews.

Ongoing monitoring of client activity

A while ago, law enforcement stopped referring to external disclosures of suspected money laundering as STRs (suspicious transaction reports) and started calling them SARs (suspicious activity reports). This is a crucial difference, as your ongoing monitoring of clients should include both their transactions and their non-transactional activity.

Monitoring transactions – i.e. money movements by your clients – is by far the simpler of the two requirements. Your firm may use an automated system to do this, or it may do manual monitoring instead. Such systems (whether automated or manual) work by matching client transactions against expected patterns and then highlighting as unusual any transactions that fall outside the predicted norm. But the legal requirement is to report *suspicious* activity, not merely *unusual* activity, and only a human being can decide whether something is actually suspicious rather than just unusual – and so every unusual transaction must be reviewed by a member of staff.

Monitoring activity is a somewhat trickier proposition than monitoring transactions. As an example, a client might contact your firm ten times in a year, changing his mailing address each time. This would not be picked up by a transaction monitoring system, as it is not a transaction, but it is activity that should be noted and perhaps considered suspicious – after all, his identity might have been compromised by a criminal who is now seeking to intercept his communications with you. Your procedures for ongoing monitoring should therefore enable you to track both transactions and non-transactional activity.

Reviews of client relationships

As well as monitoring their ongoing activity, you should also conduct regular reviews of your relationships with your clients. Your firm's RBA will determine how frequently you should do this. In short, you will be reviewing your more risky client files more frequently and your less risky client files less frequently. Schedule 3 does not specify a recommended interval, so your firm's CDD procedures will tell you what is appropriate for clients in your various risk categories.

When you review a client's file, you should ask yourself: "If this client had come to me today, in this form, is this the CDD information that I would have asked for? Or, had I known then what I know now, would I have asked for more information, or different information?" In other words, is the CDD that you hold on the client still appropriate and proportionate to the money laundering risk now presented by that client? If it is not, then you must make it so by redoing and/or adding to the CDD already on file.

Your reviews should also check for changes, such as a change of name or of signatory, or of the risk ranking of the jurisdictions involved, or in the products and services used by that client. All of this can affect the risk category that you have previously assigned to the client, and therefore the level of CDD that you must do, and the frequency and intensity with which you monitor and review them in the future.

As mentioned in the section above on *Sanctions*, you should also check the client against the current sanctions list(s) – they may have become sanctioned since you took them on as a client.

You should also check to see whether they have become a PEP (in which case, you will need to boost the CDD you have on them) or stopped being a PEP (in which case, you may be able to reduce the frequency and intensity of their monitoring and reviews).

Note here anything you would like to check in your firm's **CDD** procedures or to ask the MLCO about **CDD**:

6 RECORD-KEEPING

The second of the four components of your firm's AML regime is record-keeping, and it is perhaps the simplest of the four. In essence, your firm must keep adequate and compliant records of every aspect of its AML regime so that it can assist with money laundering investigations, as well as prove that it has complied with the requirements of Schedule 3, and offer a defence to any criminal charges of money laundering or terrorist financing.

With regard to AML records, Schedule 3 states that:

- records relating to client relationships (including CDD information, risk assessments and transaction records) must be kept for five years from the date of the end of your relationship with that client

- records relating to one-off transactions (where no relationship is established with the client beyond that one transaction) must be kept for five years from the date of completion of the transaction

- internal and external disclosures of suspicion relating to a client relationship must be kept for five years from the date of the end of your relationship with that client

- internal and external disclosures of suspicion relating to a one-off transaction must be kept for five years from the date of completion of the transaction

- training records must be kept for five years from the date of the training

- any other records pertaining to your AML regime (e.g. Board minutes, MLCO reports) must be kept for five years from the date on which they were finalised.

Several formats are permissible for these records – including paper (originals or certified copies), microfiche and scanned documents – and your firm's CDD procedures will specify what is appropriate and how such records are to be stored.

File notes

As well as keeping specific CDD documents for each client, you should also keep full and accurate file notes (preferably contemporaneous ones) as these serve to put flesh on the skeleton.

The purpose of file notes is to join the dots between the documents – to explain who made what decision, when and why. You cannot entrust such information to memory (your memory fades, and of course if you leave the firm your successors will still need access to the information), so always make fulsome file notes and then sign and date them (or the electronic equivalent). The information may be crucial during an investigation – particularly if your own conduct and compliance is under scrutiny.

Record-keeping and data protection

Under the Data Protection (Bailiwick of Guernsey) Law, 2017, your firm has obligations with regard to data collection and retention. Among other things, you need to make sure that the "personal data" you hold on clients is accurate, up to date, kept only for as long as it is needed, and kept securely. Personal data could, in theory, include internal or external disclosures of suspicion of money laundering or terrorist financing.

As the data protection legislation also allows individuals to request access to the data held on them by institutions such as firms providing fiduciary services, you can see a problem brewing: if you reveal a disclosure to a client – or even reveal the fact that the disclosure exists – you risk committing the money laundering offence of tipping off. Your firm's record-keeping procedures will have been designed with this concern in mind, and this is yet another reason why it is vital that you follow them closely. If you do not (for example, if you file a copy of a disclosure on the client file), things could go badly wrong for you and for the firm.

Note here anything you would like to check in your firm's **record-keeping** procedures or to ask the MLCO about **record-keeping**:

7 INTERNAL REPORTING

The third of the four components of your firm's AML regime is internal reporting. This is where staff are required to report any suspicions of money laundering or terrorist financing to their MLRO. Reporting such suspicions is a legal duty, it provides a defence to several of the money laundering and terrorist financing offences, it provides the Financial Intelligence Service (FIS) and others with crucial information, and indeed you should remember that failure to disclose suspicion is an offence.

You may be understandably a bit reluctant to report suspicions to your MLRO. You may worry that you are making a fuss about nothing (although such a suspicion is rarely "nothing"). You may find the reporting process confusing (although hopefully you will soon see that it is not). You may fear that you will have to defend your suspicion in court (you will not; that is another of the duties of the MLRO). Or you may simply feel that saying "I think our client may be a criminal" is just too scary (which it is – but nonetheless you must do it when the need arises).

This book cannot go into the specifics of your firm's procedures, but there are certain elements of internal reporting that are common to all firms providing fiduciary services, and it is usually a fairly straightforward process:

- There will be an internal disclosure form (either paper or electronic) which requires you to give the name and other details of the client, the date, your own name and department, and – crucially – your reason for suspecting money laundering or terrorist financing.

- You should complete this form with as much detail as you can, and forward it promptly to the MLRO.

- You should not make a copy of your disclosure, as having extra copies floating around creates an unnecessary risk of tipping off – the only copy of your disclosure should go directly to the MLRO.

- You should not share or clear your disclosure with your own manager, the client relationship manager or anyone else, regardless of any usual reporting lines. Again, this is because of the danger of tipping off: until the MLRO makes his own enquiries, you cannot be certain that other people in your firm are not involved in the suspected money laundering or terrorist financing.

- When the MLRO receives your disclosure, he will start his own enquiries to ascertain whether there is an explanation for what has happened (you may not be party to all the information concerning the client, and the MLRO will try to get the full picture) or whether there remains a suspicion of money laundering or terrorist financing.

- The MLRO will send you a receipt, so that you have proof that you complied with your legal obligations by making a disclosure – the receipt will give the date on which you made the disclosure and a unique disclosure number which ties up with the MLRO's files, but it will not mention the client's name (to guard against tipping off).

When the MLRO makes an external disclosure to the FIS, he does so online and using a specific form determined by legislation. Your internal reporting form will be modelled on that external disclosure form, so that from the very outset the MLRO is gathering the information that he may need to pass on to the FIS.

Suspicion

One of the biggest hurdles that people face when it comes to reporting suspicion is that they are not quite certain whether what they are feeling is actually suspicion. As suspicion is an emotion and therefore personal, it can be difficult to give any hard and fast definitions.

You may find it helpful to think of a "spectrum of concern", like this:

curiosity → *unease* → *doubt* → *concern* → **suspicion** → *belief* → *knowledge*

You should also remember that, thanks to the personal nature of suspicion, it does not have to be shared: just because person A is suspicious it does not mean that person B should be, and just because person B is not suspicious it does not mean that person A should not be.

For instance, you might be uneasy about something that a client does, and so you discuss it with a colleague. (The tipping off offence does not stop you doing this; it kicks in once you are suspicious, and if you are only *uneasy* you are not yet *suspicious*.) After your discussions, you find that you have now moved from unease to suspicion; your colleague, on the other hand, is not worried. It would be very foolish (not to say potentially criminal) of you not to report your suspicion on the basis that your colleague is not suspicious. You should have confidence in your own interpretation of a situation, and not be put off taking action just because no-one else seems to share your concerns. Having a suspicion of money laundering or terrorist financing and not reporting it is a serious offence.

The legal obligation is actually quite simple: if you are suspicious, you must make a disclosure.

Post-disclosure behaviour

Once you have made a disclosure, you will need to adjust your behaviour. Most importantly, you must not tell anyone that you have made a disclosure. If your colleagues need to know, so that the client relationship can be managed wisely, the MLRO will decide who can be told, when and how.

You will probably also be required to get permission from the MLRO before processing further business with the client, or before ending the relationship with the client.

Crucially, you must also continue to report anything the client does that makes you suspicious, even if it is exactly the same as the activity you reported the first time round: your original disclosure is not a blanket disclosure that covers all future transactions and activity by that client. If the MLRO decides that he has heard enough about the situation, he will let you know – but until he does, you keep on reporting.

Note here anything you would like to check in your firm's **internal reporting** procedures or to ask the MLRO about **internal disclosures**:

8 STAFF TRAINING

The last of the four components of your firm's AML regime is staff training. What your MLRO is aiming to have in place is a training programme that sensitises staff to money laundering issues without terrifying or overwhelming them or inducing paranoia, and that tells them about the firm's in-house procedures for CDD, record-keeping and internal reporting.

Who will be trained

Schedule 3 requires firms providing fiduciary services to train their "relevant employees, and any partners in the business", which may well be all of their staff. It is perfectly acceptable – and indeed expected by the GFSC – for the firm to vary the level of training to match the staff, with (for example) more detailed training being given to client-facing staff and a less detailed overview to back office staff.

Ongoing refresher training must also be provided regularly (at least every two years), to revise key points, to update you on AML issues and developing areas of criminal activity, and to give you the opportunity to raise questions and concerns.

Specific tailored training must be given to those who have particular AML responsibilities, i.e. the MLCO, MLRO and nominated officer, and the Board and senior management.

It is a condition of your employment that you attend the training provided for you. And indeed you should take the opportunity to learn more about money laundering and about the fight against it and your role in that, and to quiz the MLCO on anything that has been worrying you – after all, he is there primarily to support you in your AML efforts.

Assessing the effectiveness of staff training

Nowadays, firms providing fiduciary services are expected to be able to demonstrate that their AML training has been effective – i.e. that it has achieved the aims it was intended to achieve. Your MLCO may wish to talk to you about your training once you have completed it, or there may be a post-training quiz about what you have learned. You should not be nervous about any assessment that may take place; the point of it is not to test you, but rather to test the training.

Awareness

As well as formal staff training, you will be given AML information in other formats.

Your firm has an AML manual, either on paper or on the firm's intranet. It may be part of a larger compliance manual, and it will contain your firm's AML policy and procedures. You should make sure that you know where to find the latest version of this manual, so that you can consult it at any time. And if there is anything in there that you do not understand, or if anything is missing, you should raise this with the MLCO so that the manual can be improved.

Your MLCO might also send you email updates on money laundering matters (such as news stories, or changes to legislation), or perhaps hold informal briefings on key issues. Again, if you can, you should take every opportunity to improve your understanding of the AML effort and your role in it.

Note here anything you would like to check in your firm's **staff training** procedures or to ask the MLCO about **staff training**:

9 DISCLOSURE TO THE FIS

Your firm's in-house AML procedures are part of Guernsey's AML regime, but it is important to put them into context so that you can see how the whole process works. And a vital part of that process is the handling of reported suspicions of money laundering and terrorist financing; after all, although the aim is to prevent such crime in the first place, it is always going to happen and so there must be procedures in place to investigate it and bring those involved to justice.

Once your firm's MLRO receives an internal disclosure of suspicion, he starts making his own enquiries to enable him to decide whether or not to pass on the suspicion to the FIS in the form of an external disclosure.

The FIS – the Financial Intelligence Service – is what is known as a Financial Intelligence Unit (FIU), and most countries have one to perform just this function: the receipt and analysis of disclosures (which are often called suspicious activity reports, or SARs). The FIS is part of the Guernsey Border Agency (which makes sense, as money laundering and terrorist financing are cross-border crimes), and it is staffed by officers and civilians with police and customs expertise.

The "wrong" sort of disclosure

If a firm providing fiduciary services makes an external disclosure to the FIS and that disclosure is of the correct standard (a sensible, suspicion-based disclosure of suspected money laundering or terrorist financing, made in good faith), then the reporting firm is protected by law from being sued by its client – the subject of the disclosure – for breach of client confidentiality.

If, however, the external disclosure is not up to this standard, then that protection falls away and the firm can be sued, as the client may well be able to show that his private information was shared with the FIS in a manner not in accordance with legal requirements. It is therefore essential that only sensible, suspicion-based disclosures, made in good faith, are submitted to the FIS, and it is the responsibility of the MLRO to make sure that all of his external disclosures attain this high standard.

Consent requests

The majority of external disclosures made to the FIS are of the regular sort, where an MLRO is saying, "We have seen this happen and we think it's suspicious". However, a small proportion of external disclosures are made by MLROs asking for consent in advance of doing something: "We have been asked to do something, and we think it might be suspicious – are we permitted to do it?" These are known as consent requests, and the FIS treats them as a priority.

For instance, a firm providing fiduciary services might receive a call from a client saying that he wishes to create a trust naming several close personal friends as beneficiaries. If that seems suspicious – for instance, the client's alleged friends are all based in high-risk jurisdictions with which the client has had no previous link – the MLRO can make a consent request to the FIS before the activity has taken place. The FIS will then consider the request and either give consent or refuse it.

If you make a consent request to your MLRO and he in turn makes a consent request to the FIS, he will manage the situation carefully for you, tracking the progress of his request with the FIS and making sure that you know what you can and cannot say to the client during any delay.

What happens to external disclosures

Once the FIS receives a disclosure, it is logged onto their database, and first steps are taken to identify any links with existing information held on that database. Under careful supervision, the information in the database can be shared with other agencies to assist with all manner of investigations. The FIS will also search their database on behalf of other agencies, often overseas, in response to requests for assistance. This means that the information supplied in disclosures in Guernsey can be used to prosecute crimes other than money laundering, and to support prosecutions almost anywhere in the world.

More and more frequently, disclosures are being used to help prosecute known criminals for money laundering offences, when the police have been unable to bring successful prosecutions against them for the predicate crimes (the crimes that generated the money in the first place).

One of the most high-profile examples of this was Terry Adams, head of the Clerkenwell Crime Syndicate in London. Police had tried for years to secure convictions against him for his many unpleasant activities, among them extortion, drug trafficking, bribery, serious assault and murder. However, the fearsome reputation of Terry and of his brothers Tommy and Patsy meant that few victims were willing to talk to the police, and certainly none was prepared to give evidence in court. And then in 2007 Terry was convicted of a specimen charge of money laundering, as he was unable to prove any legal provenance for his large fortune and fancy possessions, and he was sent to prison for seven years. In 2014 he was ordered to repay £650,000 in criminal proceeds; in December 2017 he finally coughed up about £725,000, and in February 2019 he paid back an additional £50,000 in court costs accrued during his money laundering trial.

FIS case studies involving successful disclosures

Closer to home, a couple of case studies from a typologies report published by the FIS demonstrate the vital importance of this information to the wider law enforcement community.

DISCLOSURE TO THE FIS

In the first, the FIS received an alert about a man who was using a company fraudulently to promote investments allegedly with a major international bank. The company would contact people by email, offering investment opportunities with temptingly high (and frankly unrealistic) returns. Anyone who showed interest was asked to send their money to the company's bank accounts – one of which was in Guernsey. Local investigations then revealed two personal accounts in the name of the main suspect, and two business accounts in the name of the company with balances totalling £1.34 million. The FIS had received a disclosure concerning these accounts, which they shared with the investigating force in the UK. A restraining order was served locally, and the accounts are now subject to possible confiscation depending on the outcome of the UK court case.

And in the second, the FIS received a disclosure about a financial professional based in Hong Kong since 1995 who had been accused of defrauding several investors out of substantial amounts of money. The information in the disclosure was shared with the Hong Kong authorities, who then approached Guernsey with a request for mutual assistance to obtain evidential information concerning the suspect's Guernsey account. They explained that he had deceived people – including his own wife, father-in-law and friends – into investing in schemes based on gold, silver, oil, European real estate, and equity markets, and promising returns of up to 70%. He had made £1.7 million through his fraud, by not investing the money at all but using it to pay off debts and live a luxury lifestyle.

Aided by the evidence supplied by Guernsey, the authorities in Hong Kong jailed the man for eight years.

Note here anything you would like to ask the MLRO about **external disclosure to the FIS**:

10 RED FLAGS AND CASE STUDIES

One of the most challenging and fascinating features of money laundering is that it is constantly changing. Every day, criminals think of new ways to get their dirty money into and move it around the financial system. This is why it is nigh on impossible to say, "This is what money laundering looks like". However, you can look out for warning signs – red flags, as they are often called – which would prompt you to take a closer look at something. And studying known cases of money laundering is always a useful way to learn more about how criminals think and operate.

Red flags

Red flags almost all have the same thing in common: they are incidents that are out of keeping with what you expect. The words to keep in mind are *unexpected*, *unusual* and *abnormal*. If a client's activity (and remember that "activity" includes both transactions and non-transactional things) is not expected, usual and normal for that client, you should take a closer look. There may well turn out to be a good explanation for what is going on, something to clarify why the client has deviated from the expected pattern of activity, but you will not know what that explanation is unless you check. And if there is not a good explanation, this may form the first inkling of a suspicion.

It is impossible to list everything that could be construed as unexpected, unusual or abnormal (for that client, remember – so your perception will vary according to the client and what you know about them), but some common red flags for the fiduciary sector are these:

- transactions of a size, type or frequency out of keeping with what is normal for that client

- activity of a type or frequency out of keeping with what is normal for that client

- the opening and rapid closing of accounts, particularly if by clients who are connected to each other in some way

- accounts opened in, or operated through, jurisdictions with which the client has no obvious connection

- transactions or activity involving high risk jurisdictions (such as those known for poor AML regimes, or those listed in Appendix H or Appendix I to the GFSC *Handbook*, or those which are home to large numbers of sanctioned individuals and entities)

- transactions involving little-known, "Mickey Mouse" banks, professional firms or other institutions

- clients who don't seem to care about high fees or penalties, or who don't do what they can to get the best value out of your services – we know that money launderers are willing to pay up to 25% of their money to ease its way through the financial system

- unexpected loans from trusts, and subsequent repayments

- extensive use of cash and other anonymous instruments, where this is out of keeping with what you know about the client and his business

- use of third party payments, unless they are normal and expected for that client

- use of overly-complex (especially international) structures and arrangements, particularly if the client is unwilling – or unable – to explain the rationale behind them

- payment by the client of "consultancy fees" to companies established in jurisdictions known to permit the formation of shell companies

- requests to accept cash deposits into your firm's client account

- inappropriate use of your firm's client account, perhaps with movements outside what is necessary and normal

- payments into your firm's client account from an unexpected source, e.g. payment by third party cheque or remittance from an account in a jurisdiction that you were not expecting

- clients who are evasive, nervous or belligerent during normal due diligence enquiries

- clients who seem particularly interested in how serious your firm is about complying with its AML obligations.

Just to reiterate: this list is by no means exhaustive, and every situation must be assessed on its own merits and against the background of the specific client and what you know about them and their business. What you must not do is spot something that seems to you to be unusual, unexpected or abnormal, and then ignore it.

> At the end of this chapter is a blank box for you to note down any additional red flags that occur to you.

Case studies

You can open any newspaper or news website on almost any day and find a story about money laundering. Thanks to the stiff penalties on offer, and the growing experience of law enforcement agencies in successfully investigating and prosecuting money laundering, it has become very much the norm for criminals to be charged with both their original crime and laundering the proceeds of that crime. Reading about criminals and their laundering techniques is an excellent way to improve your understanding of the subject.

Thomas Scragg: tax fraudster and money launderer

Between 2002 and 2007, Solihull businessman Thomas Scragg and his business partner Paul Phillips set up several payroll companies to collect PAYE payments and VAT from contractors in the construction industry. In fact, the contractors' workmen would be paid cash in hand, and over five years the pair defrauded HM Revenue and Customs of over £26 million.

Scragg was a man of extravagant tastes. He collected sports memorabilia, including Wayne Rooney's football boots from the 2007 FA Cup final, a signed Maradona football shirt and a pair of boxing gloves signed by Leon Spinks. He splashed out on diamond and Rolex watches and drove a Bentley, and before long people started to talk about his ostentatious habits. HMRC took a closer look at him, and in November 2010 Scragg was sentenced to thirteen years in prison and Phillips to nine. Yet even as the investigators were closing in Scragg had continued his fraud, setting up more payroll companies to defraud HMRC of a further £8 million in PAYE payments between April 2007 and February 2008, and so in May 2011 four more years were added to his sentence.

After a terrifying kidnapping in 2005 in which he was tortured with a machete Scragg had decided that he needed protection, and he turned to infamous Wolverhampton brothers Carl and Anthony Johnson, paying them a total of £2.4 million in protection money. And in a fine example of the money laundering legislation being used to convict people against whom others are too frightened to testify, in July 2012 the

Johnson brothers were each sent to prison for two years and nine months for laundering the proceeds of Scragg's fraud by accepting payments from him.

There were many others involved in laundering Scragg's criminal proceeds. Investigations showed that Scragg had transferred large amounts – up to £70,000 a day – to a money services business in Solihull called Cash 4 Cheques. The owner of the business, George White, then paid cash out to Scragg – £3.6 million in total between April 2007 and February 2008 – and was sentenced to 2½ years in prison for money laundering. Chartered accountant and tax adviser Bruce Hartle helped White to run Cash 4 Cheques and gave Scragg tax advice; he was given thirty months for money laundering. Alfred Namutulo ran an accountancy business called Namusti & Co, and he became the auditor for some of Scragg's payroll companies. He helped apply for a "dispensation" from HMRC that he advised Scragg would cover up the fraud, as well as producing and submitting false documents to HMRC; he was jailed for six years. Scragg's luxury possessions were sold at police auction in December 2013, with the proceeds going to public projects.

Beano Levene: fraudster and money launderer

Nicholas "Beano" Levene – the nickname came from his love of the children's comic – was a successful London financier. After emigrating to Israel with his family when he was fifteen, Levene served in the Israeli military and worked as a hotel bellboy before returning to England and finding his niche in the City. At the age of 21, and at the peak of the 1980s boom, he started trading and quickly earned a fortune.

A popular man, with the gift of the gab, Levene used his contacts and strong reputation to win over people with talk of seemingly concrete investment deals from which he would take a commission or fee. Between 2005 and 2009, he took millions of pounds from high-profile people – including Richard Caring (owner of The Ivy and Le Caprice restaurants in London) and Russell Bartlett (director of the R3 Investment Group and former owner of Hull City Football Club) – promising to invest for them in lucrative rights-issue releases from companies such as HSBC, Lloyds TSB, Xstrata and Rio Tinto which (he claimed) were unattainable for ordinary investors. But instead he spent most of the money on gambling, cars (including one with the number-plate B3ANO), yachts, property and parties.

Things started to unravel in 2009. Sir Brian Souter and his sister Ann Gloag (founders of Stagecoach) had each given Levene £5 million to invest in Xstrata and HSBC. When they made £3.8 million each they instructed him to sell, but they never received either their capital or the profit – and took him to court. A second writ, claiming £720,000 plus interest, then came from spread betting firm IG Index; Levene had lost that sum gambling on a Twenty20 cricket match between South Africa and the West Indies in September 2007. On 7 October 2009 Levene was declared bankrupt, and the Serious Fraud Office launched an investigation into his finances while Levene himself checked into the Priory Clinic for treatment for his gambling addiction.

Over the period in question, Levene took £32,352,270 from investors – but, taking into account the lost profits on those investments, investigators declared the total value of the Ponzi fraud to be £101,685,406. (A Ponzi fraud is where you use money from new investors to pay enough returns to keep existing investors happy, all the while recruiting new investors. When you cannot find enough new investors to provide the required returns, the scheme will collapse.)

Addressing Levene prior to sentencing in court in November 2012, Judge Martin Beddoe referred to the financier's "rank dishonesty" and said: "You were responsible for a fraud on a massive scale with a huge panoply of aggravating features, well planned and professionally executed, involving huge sums and huge profits with multiple victims whose trust in you was grossly abused. It was committed over a long period, was well concealed and you took further steps to conceal it and further steps to hide profits from it." Levene was jailed for thirteen years for fraud, false accounting and money laundering. In March 2013, he was ordered to repay £1 – a nominal sum set by the court in light of his bankruptcy.

Curtis Warren: drug dealer and money launderer

Born in Liverpool in 1963, Curtis Warren is a career criminal. He graduated swiftly from car theft to armed robbery and then to drug trafficking. He laundered the £20 million cash proceeds from his drug business using a simple technique called "smurfing": he instructed drug addicts to pay small amounts of cash into dozens of firm accounts and then rewarded them with drugs. He also set up a string of small, cash-intensive businesses in Liverpool so that he could pay even more cash into the financial system. In 1992 Warren was finally charged with trafficking 907kg of cocaine into the UK for the Colombian Cali cartel, but he had to be freed when it was revealed that his partner in crime was a police informant.

Threatened by rival drug dealers, Warren moved to the Netherlands. By now, he owned hundreds of properties, including an English football ground, Spanish casinos, Turkish discos and a Bulgarian vineyard. He appeared in the *Sunday Times* "Rich List" in 1998, with his profession given as "property developer". Dutch police watched him carefully – their job made more tricky by his photographic memory, which meant that he never needed to write anything down – and eventually they caught him shipping Colombian cocaine to his Bulgarian vineyard, dissolving it in the wine, and then shipping the bottles to the Netherlands for the cocaine to be distilled out and sold. He was sent to prison in the Netherlands for twelve years – but the majority of his fortune could not be traced.

Just three weeks after his release from prison in June 2007, Warren travelled to Jersey. He was now under constant surveillance, having been made subject to the UK's "lifetime offender management programme". In Jersey he met up with another man, and bugging of their calls revealed that they were plotting with a contact in Amsterdam to smuggle drugs into Jersey. After some legal wrangling, Warren was sentenced to thirteen years in prison, to be served in London.

After extensive investigations into the location and source of Warren's financial assets (he claimed to run a fruit and veg stall on a Liverpool market), in November 2013 the Royal Court of Jersey ordered him to repay £198 million of criminal proceeds within 28 days. The money was not forthcoming, and so Warren was ordered to serve another ten years in prison – with the money still owing.

Note here any **red flags** that you would like to add to the list:

11 USEFUL SOURCES OF INFORMATION

Your MLCO is your best source of current money laundering and AML information, but some of the most commonly referenced websites are these:

Financial Action Task Force (FATF)	www.fatf-gafi.org
Financial Intelligence Service	www.guernseyfis.gg/
Guernsey AML/CFT legislation and guidance	www.gfsc.gg/commission/financial-crime/legislation-and-guidance
HM Treasury Office of Financial Sanctions Implementation	www.gov.uk/government/organisations/office-of-financial-sanctions-implementation

MONEYVAL	www.coe.int/moneyval
Office of Foreign Assets Control sanctions page	www.treasury.gov/resource-center/sanctions/Pages/default.aspx
States of Guernsey sanctions website	www.gov.gg/sanctions

ABOUT THE AUTHOR

Susan has worked in the anti-money laundering field for more than twenty years. In 2003 she set up Thinking about Crime Limited, a dedicated anti-money laundering consultancy. Her services include the provision of anti-money laundering training to staff and Money Laundering Reporting Officers, the reviewing and writing of anti-money laundering policies and procedures, and the undertaking of AML audits to assess the effectiveness and compliance of in-house AML regimes. As a trained teacher with an all-consuming interest in (some might say obsession with) money laundering, Susan is ideally placed to design and deliver training and procedures that are compliant, effective and, yes, even enjoyable.

If you have any questions, please email Susan:
susan@thinkingaboutcrime.com

Or why not join in the discussions on her blog:
www.ihatemoneylaundering.wordpress.com

If you have enjoyed this book, why not relax after work with one of Susan's novels, all dealing with financial crime in London in the 1820s

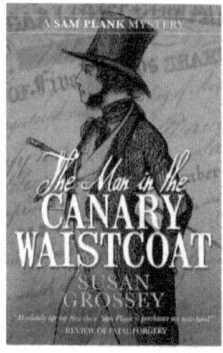

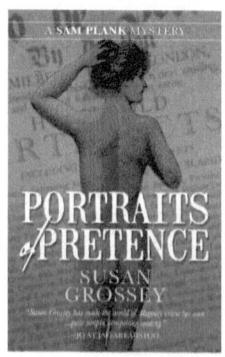

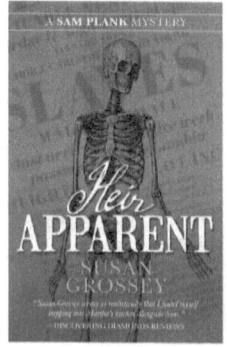

USEFUL SOURCES OF INFORMATION